The Vigorous
Lifestyle of Dating

The Vigorous Lifestyle of Dating

Calvin B. Shivers

authorHOUSE®

AuthorHouse™
1663 Liberty Drive
Bloomington, IN 47403
www.authorhouse.com
Phone: 1-800-839-8640

Published by AuthorHouse   04/04/2012

ISBN: 978-1-4685-4937-9 (sc)
ISBN: 978-1-4685-4941-6 (e)

Library of Congress Control Number: 2012902784

Chapter-1

Dating

If you have a date with a lady you just met from one of the dating sites, and you exchange phone numbers. When the following Monday arrive and you decide to give her a call to express your gratitude for the wonderful time spent together at the restaurant and movies. If she doesn't respond to your verbal or texted messages that you sent. Make it a three day rule not to call her until that coming Thursday of the week. If she still don't respond chalk it up as a learning experience and move on, no doubt she probably has a man on the side or she's simply not interested in you.

Chapter-2

<u>Never Date</u>

When a woman has three or more children expect drama, any woman with that many kids is not looking for a serious relationship. Unless it's with the kids farther, and since that's not going to happen any time ever considering their past. You might want to find a woman with less luggage, like one or two kids where the mother has more control. If not, and you continue dating this kind of woman with three or more kids. You will only find yourself helping her keep food in her refrigerator paying most of her bills, and babysitting her badass kids if they are not of age to watch themselves. My suggestion to you is run, run as fast as you can and try to stay away from women with kids.

Chapter-3

Contact

A physical attraction is one the most psychological traits of the human species, which is a curiosity in us based on our emotion that we feel. People are attracted to one another by sight when we show interest in who we see and what we like. Singles dating has become more sexual than inhibited, expressing what we want inspite of our plans of what we need. It consumes us of the possibilities on what we all have become considering the facts about how we live our lives.

Chapter-4

The Hunt

In the mood for love, just like shopping for a car a women have her own unique characteristics. What a man look for in viewing a woman shape, size, eye's and smile, with certain facial features that appeal to our sense of taste in the kind of woman we would like to have. While seeing these women on a computer screen we cannot determine what her behavior pattern is like by a simple profile. However, in most cases we can chat online and send messages only to find some women with screwed up attitudes and mixed up minds whenever they present themselves as real. They come off like they are so interested in you then like a child in candy store they want everything that's meant be to ordered, what a slut; However, each woman is different in their action as far as finding a man and most are truly looken to find a compatible mate depending on the nature of her social involvement.

Chapter-5

High Impact

The first barrier in getting next to a women is improachment, taking gradual steps to advance beyond the brick walls she has put up over her past relationships. Don't come off with a line like some young teenager having one thing in mind. Just be yourself without violating her right of space, always be polite when making your intention clear. Let her know you are available and ask if she is single. A key method of phrase is I like what I see; No matter what her response is you are sure to get a smile with an indication if she is interested in you or not.

Chapter-6

Show Confidence

Choose a woman that is compatible to you, make sure she is the type of lady that you like and want her to be. When a women is not willing to go that extra mile for her man, this is a very selfish person by nature, and considering the type of woman that she is. You will never have a meaningful relationship with a woman of her character. Instincts should tell you to get rid of her immediately without any hesitation discontinue any involvement with a woman like her.

Chapter-7

Do It in Moderation

When assessing what you want out of your relationship, don't ever let money become an issue when considering things to do with your date. However, you can look for things to do without spending your life savings. The main goal here is just to have a good time with your date even if it's just walking in the park.

Chapter-8

Dress To Impress

Always dress your best when out looking for women to meet, a new pair of shoes, paints, and shirt among other attire will have all women swarming at your feet. Please don't take this literally this is just a figure of speech, besides women love it when men dress nice.

Chapter-9

Hygiene Means Everything

Don't ever leave your place or residents without taking a bath or shower especially when you're going to meet your date, as mom once said," You never know who you might see". So always comb your hair, and brush your teeth and don't forget to use deodorant.

Chapter-10

Being Stood Up

When you have met someone over the internet or by phone, don't take it personal if they don't show up. It could have been a number of reasons why, with good reason. Always give your date the benefit of the doubt, and find out the reason why they didn't show if you can. Never assume the worst and consider the impossible; if you have called them more than five time to show your concern about their whereabouts. If they don't respond, then nine times out ten you have been stood up. Move on for the best is yet to come, and she is probably not for you any way.

Chapter-11

Most Impressive

A gentlemen brings roses or flowers on a first date, which show his decore of class from a high impact specialist opposite of all scenarios an techniques. Dinner is fine, but make sure you let her choose, women can appreciate a man that lets her take the lead. Unless she insist you take charge always remain flexible generalization is the key. If you're ever in doubt where to take your date try Chinese, it's affordable and it makes for a good conversation piece.

Chapter-12

Never Talk About Past Relationships

For most women they prefer not to bring up past relationships, which is a topic that shouldn't cross a man lips. The reason are very clear in one way or another, women like a man that focuses all his attention on her, and not the sour past relationship of other females you been with. Let her see the light shining in you expressing your superiority of success of not dwelling in your past, and never ask a woman about her past relationship unless she divulges it. Women tend to find men less attractive when they talks about other women.

Chapter-13

Be Honest With Your Date

Right from the beginning, be honest with your date. Let her know your likes and dislikes, and what you want out of the relationship you look forward to having with her. A man's character plays a big part in his role as a man a woman can trust. His sincerity is the quality he displays's base on what he says, and his actions. Besides being genuine and honest pretty much will tell how good a new relationship will go.

Chapter-14

Sexual Exploits

I can have my cake and eat it too when it comes to this endless pleasure of ecstasy. This can either work with you or against you depending on the type of woman that you go for. When dealing with women that are very horney, nemphos by sexual origin it becomes more business than relationship. Most men that are more into the business types of women are looking for a more liberal kind of woman, you know the kind that wears the dress suites with short skirts or pants with the high heels pumps. This really gets the average mans attention when you're out on the scene painting your way for a night out on the town.

Chapter-15

Idle Conversation

Idle conversation is good during lunch or dinner with your date talking about the weather or everything else in between. This will give you insight into how comfortable your date is around you. This will determine the outcome of the date if it is to continue. You will know by the end of your date if she is interested in you, or will blow you off by telling you she has things to do before you can even get your foot in the door. This could mean she feels no connection with you at all, but may like you as a friend but not enough to have a genuine relationship with you. You are just not her type.

Chapter-16

What To Look For
In Body Language

Eye contact is one of the most important symbols of body language, any type of fidgeting or constant body movement is a sure sign that your date is not comfortable with you or her settings. In any case there is no connection when her body language say's it all, best case scenario move on.

Chapter-17

A Woman's Insecurities

When dealing with a woman insecurities always consider her feelings, remember she is very sensitive when it comes to her looks, weight, clothes, hair and shoes. Women always want to look their best when ever out in the public eye, so any jokes about the way she looks or inappropriate statement about her job etcetra. Is a no no, this will send up red flags about your character thumbs down. Which means the end of your date and you, key words hold your tongue.

Chapter-18

Dating Online
Supposedly Single Women

In all retrospect you are really flipping a coin, when it comes to dating women online. The majority of these women have men they either live with or already seeing, and they call us sick. Most of them on the sites are so badly damaged, battered and bruised, with mental challenges it's a wonder they date at all. Their sense of direction is a road map to destruction from the physical and mental abuse that they suffer. So you men out there really have to be careful, when dating women on the sites. They act as if they're perfect, lost between the words been here forever and still looking. Still stuck and alone without a good man to eat her cooken, if she can cook at all. What I have learned most about these kind of women, if I learned anything at all, and that's don't take them to lunch or dinner and if you do don't forget to bring a doggy bag.

Chapter-19

Indication Of Not Interested

Women have very clever ways of letting guy's know they're not interested in them. In passing they either don't look at you or pretend they don't see you at all, how rude. Some women go as far as putting their heads and eye's upward as if to be looking up into the sky, or facing straight ahead as if she's lost in a trance. That's when you really know there is nothing happening, so remember the many signs of women looks. So when you men are looking for a date, if she's interested in you she will strike up a conversation with you guaranteed.

Chapter-20

The More Subtle Approach

There are all kind of approaches to score with a woman, and there are plenty of chances of being turn down. The more suddle approach seems to always work best for me this has been the most successful one of all. When you walk up to the lady of your dreams and introduce yourself offering a service of whatever she wants to drink at the bar you'll pay. It never fails, let her know that you are interested her and leave your number on her tits when you're finished. If you did a good job from the night before she will call you again. If she don't move on to the next one for the propositions are endless just like the women you seek.

Chapter-21

Stay Away From Fake Bitches

(1) How can you tell a fake bitch is by the way she dresses with her cheap made perfume, and her runny mascara. Mentally unattached and a fucked up attitude with a loss of common sense. (2) The way she walks is as if she has four dicks ram up her ass, instead of having a sway she limps with a twist, maybe it's because all the guy's she fucked with stiff long dicks. Stuck so far up her ass hitting every other hole available. Imagine when she shopping or going to get her hair and nails done. When she walks into the salon she move with a stride instead of a glide, with pussy fatter than a snach now try to imagine that. (3) She always act as if she is in a hurry all the time never slowing down until her butt hit each curb, funky with her ways just another pretty face. (4) Fake contact lenses and much much more money grubing little bitches is a dick best friend. (5) A man pretty much has to be able to dissect an analyze these type of bitches with a knife and fork, and know the differences between the two in order to know what to look for in each subject within itself, this way you can determine on how you want to judge. (6) As I take you even further into my examination of this extraordinary woman, which makes her an exceptional creature. What I have learned about these kind of women is a man cannot measure the full extent of their nature. (7) Their minds changes like the weather, if she wears to much makeup she gets a headache, her eyes hide in the

shadows when it's her time of the month. For me to mention anything else is a list to long to fill, and I pretty much covered the list of women that fall in the category of women on what to look for. They are very moody, vein, shallow in every way of genetic make up with character flaws. Watch how she gets naked and began to lick your balls.

Chapter-22

What Makes Dating So Unique

What makes dating so unique is the many different types of nationality of women you have to choose from. The women that you see from the ones you find most attractive gives a man a sense of hope in finding the right lady to be the women in his life. It become more routine than justified in what you would like to have, if and when you can make a connection. Being on most of these dating website is like having a common place, which has become for most an addiction when you see men and women with the many different smiles, styles, and looks to appeal to the others invitation of charm. I can't help but think just how lonely most of those people really are, which leaves me in thought on why can't we stay in love with the person we fell in love with. I can't help but play with the fact that men and women are thinking the same thing when you are in search of love that was there in the first place. This crosses the line when you have met that special someone that never works out, when being on the same wave link becomes a dilemma from meeting that special person that simply makes you smile.

Chapter-23

Each Woman Is Different

No two women are the same no matter how you slice it, they may stick together in most cases, but the same in a lot of ways which make them all the more special. There is a quality of giving that is measured by her quality of care (simplicity). The lack of good sense is not tolerated by a women's character of intelligence, when a man acts out she will prefer not to deal with his foolishness especially when their out on a date. If he is not acting accordingly like a gentlemen is suppose to, all red flags go up with a connection now broken. A women perception of a man conversation lets her analyze how you might treat her out in public. A woman always wants to be treated with the up most respect, with no jokes thrown in between fine lines of grandeur. This goes for no huffen, no coughing, no burps or farts, and if you're getting ready to cough make sure to cover your mouth. Keep the conversation simple and say what's on your heart, Some women are more over the same in a lot of ways, but different in action or thoughts.

Chapter-24

<u>Getting To Know Her</u>

It's easy to find out about what a woman likes and dislikes. Which don't mean following her around the grocery store to see what food she buys. A woman will tell you that information when she wants you to know it, depending on what she wants you to know. Most certainly she will want to know about you without matter of opinions to hear what you have to say about the different types of things you like to do. Only to see if any of the things you like are compatible to things she likes. Which will create a bond with you and her sharing what you have in common in order to make you her soul mate. Rather it's a art museum, walk in the park or day at the beach. Either way getting to know her is one the most important expression of feelings a man can offer a lonely woman.

Chapter-25

Trust

The most intricate part of a relationship is (trust) don't let anyone tell you anything different. Without it you have nothing worth building a solid foundation on. Practically every woman in the word is looking for financial stability, in pretty much every relationship I've been in a woman is looking for financial and moral support. Not to mention being able to counsel each other through the rough times. A man should always stand by his woman side no matter what the obstacles are as each situation manifests itself no matter how transparent it may seem.

Chapter-26

Behave Your Self

Behaving your self have to do with the type of women your dating. What I mean by that is, if she is the kind of woman raised in the city she is very hard case snappish and fast on her feet. She can become an annoyance with her remarks of curtness, subject to bite and very leery of all men. This is due to the environment she was raised and brought up in, and these women are known in cities all over the world. In my matters of opinion you would be better off with a wild country girl. Let's just say you're trying to date a lady from NYC; The crime rate is so high with the bombardment of thugs it makes it next to impossible to date a high caliber of women without her thinking you are going to rip her off. It don't matter your dress code, a thief come in many shapes forms or fashion. If you don't believe me . . . be a gentlemen and ask her if you can walk her home or at least pay for her cab, and she will look at you like your crazy and swear she knows what's up. I guess you can say there's a shortage of decent guy's in NY, without a woman thinking she might get raped purse snatched and stolen or beat up. All because she's trying to have a goodtime, so yea, I say dating a woman from the city can be a real hassle. Now country women on the other hand seem to be a lot more subtle seductive, radiant with appeal and willing to take chances. Which maybe that's because that they know everybody. They are more outgoing and willing to give a man the benefit of the doubt, depending on what part of the country you're in, where you're at and who you're with. Nine times out of ten you can best believe she has sister's, brothers, cousins, uncles, and aunts hanging somewhere around just to keep an eye on her. You will never know it unless directly introduced, they are watching over her while they are checking you out. I'm not saying southern women are better, or any less than city women; But if I had my pick of the liter city girls are on my list. All I'm saying gentlemen is to expand your search for the lady you're looking for, but remember the environment that they're in, and try to keep an open mind to the women your dating that ask a lot of question.

Chapter-27

Herpes And
Other Venereal Diseases

When your dating and meet someone for the first time you have know clue on who they been with or what they may have far as their sexual orientation, if a person is infected with some type transmitted disease. You expect them to do the right thing by telling you that they are infected, which in most cases this is not always true. A person having herpes, aids, or any other infectious disease has a responsibility rather it's a man or a woman to inform the person that their planning on having sex with, that they are infected with whatever kind of disease they have. Which is why it is always safe to wear condoms ladies and gentlemen, and important to ask a person if they have any kind of health issues regarding their sexual orientation. It's also important to ask he or she if they are on any kind of medication, and if so what is it for. Which can also determine if you want to have a relationship with this person or not. I believe every woman and man have a obligation to each other if he or she has been exposed to any venereal transmitted disease. Even the most common of symptoms like, allergies, cancers, stroke, and any other stigmas that may cause you complication to your health.

With this in mind you will be able to decide if you want that relationship with this person or not. So be honest with each other people concerning any illnesses you may have, for honest is the best medicine.

Chapter-28

Can She Be The One

There are many ways a man could explore if a woman is truly interested in him. The one most commonly known, by dating other women. When dating more than one woman it will give you the option of comparing the woman that you seek. In your analysis you will determine which one you like the most, in order to make a final decision on the one you want to spend the rest of your life with. This also gives you a chance to know what you like and dislike about each one. Fore example if one of the women your dating shows a more genuine interest in what you like to eat, drink, and the things and places you two like to go. As well as liking a lot of things that you like, far as sports, reading, camping, fishing.ect . . . Then there is definitely a connection of compatibility, then just maybe she should be the one you choose. Make absolutely sure six months into the relationship you and her both have cut all ties with any past dating partners. Those are skeletons you want to stay covered and buried forever. If you for some reason or nother still have a guy trying to hang on to your woman, it can complicate things in what you and her are trying to build far as a future together. So make it clear to her your feelings you have is for her and her alone and hope she is feeling the same way to.

Chapter-29

Women That's Been Divorced

Women that's been married and then divorced are pretty much damage goods. Dating them is okay, but having a long term relationship with them will only end up in disaster. Maybe not for all but to a certain degree, not to say every woman that's been divorced has issues in respecting a man's rights. There are a few exception, and they are far few and in between, you see the truth of the matter is when a divorced women finds a man she likes. She is constantly sizing him up for the long haul of the relationship to get married again, measuring you up for a tux she wants to see you in close to the middle of the next year in May, yep mother's day. So when you have met all of the criteria for what she wants in her man, you are definitely on her hit list, because no one wants to live alone.

Chapter-30

Clever Women

Women that are clever know how to lure a man into their circle, when she likes what she sees. The man that seeks this type of woman can best believe she won't choose you, sad as it might sound women play a lot of games, having you believing she is going to be with you then change on you in an instant. What I know from past experiences, and what it has taught me while being in different relationships with women, was what to look for in women under the impression that they are doing nothing wrong. They never take the time to consider how a man might feel when she plays with his emotion like that. Instead she probs an probes to see what buttons she can push in order to get what she want, or abuse you mentally base on how you might feel for her. Women can be very manipulative when looking to get what she wants, which is called the selfish bitch concept. Whereas the only rules she abide by is her own, so men have to prepare themselves for the riggermoroe. So as long there's indication that you can dispute her actions no matter her adversities toward you, watch out for cat claws and sex appeal.

Research Taught Me

Most older women have a tendency to want younger men depending on his character preferences, while younger women on the other hand only want to be with younger guy's based on looks toughness, and how well they perform in bed as well as the size of their dicks. Younger women look to be with order men only if he has something to offer, besides the money in his pocket or the size of his bank account. In most cases, younger women want what most older women don't want; (DRAMA). It all start with a look with what women desire far as dating is concerned; Searching in detail in choosing what she thinks might be what she wants out of her relationship. Depending on the caliber of woman, relying on the gentleness of a man to enrich her spirit for the quality of woman she might be. She wants all these things in a man that might not have any idea what she is looking for unless she tells him, whatever her intention are you pretty much have to figure them out for yourself. The majority of men main purpose in dating is getting some pussy. Why sugar coat it when all the good fella's are turning gays, and if it's meant to be young or old women they will be yours for the taken as long as women and men take the necessary precautions by letting them choose you.

Chapter-32

Give Me Some Play

How much pussy can a man get in his lifetime? The answer to the question is as much as he can to fulfill his need if ever a need to be filled. When I make a play at a woman you can best believe her pussy is on my mind, having thoughts of it is like how it will fill when I'm inside, will it be soft and juicy or dry and tight . . . with a fragrance so alluring from the perfume palmerating her skin would make any man go nutts by the shere sight of her coming out of her clothes. With much added attraction with the dress she's wearing turns men heads from down the street. I look for certain type of woman well cased to a degree of uniqueness, well versed in her conversation which leaves you hanging on her every word that she speaks. Her poise of elegance frequently unexpected wetness measuring the human instincts captures the main ingredients of songs, singing out to her moist ecstasy. I almost want to shed a tear because not only is she well versed and educated with degree's of simplicity. Her over all back ground seem more profound than coming to America; My focus is finding this kind of woman compatible to what I seek for me. I've always pride myself on the good looks of a woman that I'm dating, well not any more. Looks don't mean squat if she don't have the brains to go with it, no matter where we go she has to have that show of confidence that represent me.

Chapter-33

When Dating Two Women

The benefits of dating two women is they have showed interest in you based on what they see. The one that you choose is totally up to you, as the relationships began to blossom you eventually decide which one you are going to keep. Now depending on what you're looking for in your woman, rather it's her voluptuous body or brains to boot with a tall sexy full figured matched by long firm legs. We all fall victim under the spell of a woman's shape build with such sophistication curves of her body falls in rhythm with the shape of her ass. Oh how we love them all . . . soon they will want to share their body with you, but only if you choose one. And don't think for a second that the experienced woman don't know that she is in competition with one or more women. Especially if you are a gentleman of quality which there is no doubt in her mind she wants to be number one as the new women behind the man in style. That's why we set our standards high when it comes to marring a good quality of woman with real love of service no matter what the cost with a successful woman that consider herself practically gold in your eyes when you decide she's worth keeping for a lifetime of satisfaction.

Chapter-34

To Date With Sophistication

To date with sophistication is having the confidence to know just what you want in your mate from the moment you meet. There will be a rapport of knowing exactly what you want in that person that is non-sequential to your desire that clearly recognizes what you feel at the moment of attachment to the person you have already analyzed. This a positive affect that combines the two of you in the moment of passion allowing the opportunity for love to creep in. A women often knows what she wants when she meets a man, rather she want to be with him or not before he do. She even knows if she will sleep with him depending on his character before he is even considered, this goes beyond the path of dating opportunities that make most men optimistic. It becomes imperative expressing our action of command having the power of control in which that cannot be controlled. In a five year span of loneliness when getting back into the swing of things no man or woman fall short when it comes to finding that one special person to make their lives whole again. So we become victims of our own self indulgences, by serial dating each and every person we can, how sad. Women are the worst, desperately seeking the warmth of compassion of man a with considerable talent of appeal before realizing his cynical methods of false pretenses. This becomes more annoying than the actual disappointment of bitterness she tries so hard to conceal. This is what I call a make shift wall of bubbles with names of men that's been discarded. This evokes the mentally sick on dating sites committed to loving games with any length of time running out of relationships with people lost in a computer generated world.

Chapter-35

There Is No Secret To Dating

When you're in the main stream of dating there is bounds in disappointments. There is no secret formula's, no magic bags of tricks, no hocus pocus to make her spin or flip. Each negative experience only leaves a scar if you let it, realizing later that the women that you fell in love with is a complete basket case. This is not uncommon; you just have to remain focused on your objective in finding a woman that is suitable to your needs. Men are very vulnerable to a woman standard of thinking, subjected to her values in what she wants in the way she wants her man to be. The possibilities are endless; which leads us down the path of accountability going into a relationship without fully checking her out for disturbing behavior of her thought process. You can take it or leave it with a series of action directed to no end. How do you rectify the situation is simple, by finding someone new; "case solved".

Chapter-36

Diversify Your
Option When Dating

If you're dating two women or more, write out a scheduled list balancing the information you have on them far as their everyday activity. For instance if you have to meet them at a certain time, stay updated with their plans each day, on topic you have discussed, this will keep down confusion if you make any mistake in plans that you have made with each other. For example: If you happen to have two women get off of work at the same time that require for you to meet them at the same time at their place of origin; Then you better come up with an excuse on why you can't meet one of them, I believe it's called a lie. In any case nothing is full proof in a perfect relationships between two women no matter what kind of failsafe you think you have in order to keep both of them satisfied. The consequences always out way the normal flow of balance when decite dangles on the verge of destruction. It is an option mostly used with guys caught up in a jam, endorsed by cheaters all over the world. Exceptional maybe, but not recommended so we learn from the games we play.

Chapter-37

A Woman That's Willing To Experiment

Every relationship starts with a date when a woman's adventure remains to be seen. What starts off as a moderate casual dry eyed dinner with a few churls but no laughter, should give you an indication that there is no real connection between you two. Which leads you to believe that she is just another lame brain chick looking for Mr. perfect with a big dick, own house, own car, preferably a Benz. This type of woman is known as lady high class when it comes to certain men, looking to get all that she can from a relationship that might have some potential without disappointing setbacks. Women can become so vicious in their search for single available men, and if for some reason it don't work out they're never at a lost. With a smile that melts like ice when you look into her face of promise; having skin so silky smooth and soft, as to ride on wings with winds of fate, is just a small price to pay if she makes you her mate. When every man standing at attention just by her appearance alone lighting up the room as if she's in a dark place. She knows what she wants and how to get it.

Chapter-38

Male And Female Species

Cat and mouse the chase has begun, babies need parents in a world surrounded by predators. This is an application designed to increase the human population by the millions. Measured by the length of time two people spend together to form a union or bond in order to live more productive lives. No matter how you slice it, it becomes essential for men and women to find the person they are compatible to, based on the character of that person. Which 95% of the time the relationship never last, finding what you want just to throw it all away. On the majority of websites it's like a revolving door that never closes, always open to meet your fate. Caught in a masquerade of the many different faces of masks, welcoming performers into a circle of lies and games. This is an endless web of mazes connected to different places, which some of them you've seen before on other websites as you recognize their faces when you stopped and sent a message. A constant line of charades to see who is the best actor, women and men teams with a blatant pretense of deception. Entering a unfore seen future with no one but yourself, while you are asking her, ask yourself what do you really want. To find the lady that you desire when emotions set you up, just make sure you expand your search cause true love is hard to find.

Chapter-39

The Threat of A Predator

You have women and men from all walks of life, some in search of love, many out to ruin your life. The websites is full of predators that probe the web like sharks of different breeds, set out to get you any way they can. Financially, mentally, and physically depending on who they are. Look at what we become considering the circumstances characterized by violence, surrounding material things concrete in nature and designed by science which has become a metaphor of examples. It would seem that we are practically selling our souls to be safe by devices sold to keep us safe from the destructive people that's out to hurt you which are the very people that we trust. When all your trying to do is find a soul mate compatible to you so you can relate on a more personal bases. Some people may find it a challenge weeding out the individuals responsible for trying to create or cause drama for the purpose of making your life miserable. This is a task left without words when you don't have to wonder why they are there. This can make it hard for a man to find a good woman, and a woman to find a good man. I figure the quality of the type of person we look for is not measured by the dating sites that we choose, but the individuals that's on these sites with an enter at your own risk policy. Stay away from them fools, when a woman have to worry about if she's safe to be with you; Comes with the conversation or chat that you have with him at the point of entry which can prolong the idea of meeting someone suitable, because they have moved on to another mate. This scenario is ongoing and common by comparison when he or she steadily looks to find someone better.

Chapter-40

The Game Of Chance

This begin when a person enters in and out of romance with no substitute for the one you lost. When trying to find another for the one you lost and loved, when you do find the person you like or fall in love with, you are taking a chance on the fact that he or she will be everything you expect in them to be for the way that you feel. Now that you and this person have been communicating for about six months, and it's time to meet with an array of thoughts running through your mind. You can't help but wonder if he or she will be much better than the person you once had. Having hope that they are healthy successful and complete, which can make you all the more afraid of who they are. You can only imagine how they might feel when meeting you for the first time, other than seeing a picture of you that really don't define your character until you meet them. You try to keep your wits about you because no one can be sure about anything when wanting someone that you seek. It really makes differences on how the game is played when looking at familiar faces; the dating game can be very convincing when you don't even know their names. When all you have is a computer screen with jesters of nicknames, and faces with a few words of whom and what they're looking for in a woman or man. How you treat them with the messages perceived secure the benefits of doubts, when you treat that person accordingly from a sour life turning romantic.

Chapter-41

Out Of Touch

In many endeavors of going in and out of relationships, rather it's mental or physical past or present. A person must take a stand and time out if you will, to set your thoughts about his or her character. To access the many different facts about what you're looking for in the type of person that you choose to be with. When a man has left an abusive relationship they never give themselves time to heal from the process of the emotional conflicts he might feel. His thoughts may wonder in and out of who's right and who's wrong then try to justify his actions by doing something stupid, that he might end up in jail or dead. Instead of giving his self enough space between him and his woman to cool down by soul searching feelings of his actions far as being a man. No matter his past discrepancies with her, a man's main concern should be how he can better himself in character toward women that's a lot less argumentative and assertive in expressing her emotion's with control, by talking to her when the two of them have a disagreement. However, men have a tendency to temporarily forget about his significant other, when some good looking woman comes along and offer you the same deal you have at home, but at a different place. It's a never ending cycle when man continues to jump right back into the same relationship he just left, without taking the time to know the woman he is getting involved with. Thinking that just because she has a nice body, shape, good looks and nice personality, this will make the mistakes he made with his last girlfriend go away in what he wants in another woman. Not appealing as it may seem, it often results back into the same situation you left before. Especially if you're not working, this will lead to hardship and a multitude of emotional stress. So fella's take the time to learn how not to rush into anything that could leave you seeking help to heal your mind from the negative thoughts about women. This is a thought process that returns to the beginning on every ending that repeats itself in the same sequence when you're out of touch with yourself. So take the time out to discover self in order to stay in touch with you.

If She Is Close To Her Daddy

Much of an improvement when a father wants the best for his daughter, creating a bond that will last a life time. When a woman is close to her father she is in search of a man that has the same characteristic traits, and personality type as her father that will ensure a more established relationship between the man she chooses when dating. This will eliminate any man opposite in what she is looking for when looking to find her more suitable mate. If the man she seek don't have that same swagger with a unique appeal of vernacular decore her search could be endless, women thrive on men with confidence who's self assurance has a endless supply of merit. In women of caliber mostly it is a traditional necessity instinctively necessary to bring into her family the right man that will be approved by her father with the assurance that she has made the right choice. That among other things when she brings him to meet dear old daddy wondering if he will meet up to his expectation in what she cannot be sure in determining if she has made the right choice. This is unavoidable and maybe a little eccentric by comparison of the fact that if she is able to make up her own mind or not, without the help of her father. With this kind of depiction it's a wonder why there are so many women alone in the world today. With the consideration of the normality with labels of who and what they are hopelessly looking for, (Mr. Right) popular by demand in her confidence that he is out there somewhere she hasn't been, waiting for her to find him or vice versa.

Chapter-43

When A Woman Show Cleavage

A woman shows her cleavage to lure man to her sense of appeal, and if he has money that's even better. This will make up for it in his looks department if he has none, and if he is desirable with good looks and a strong muscular physique that expresses his full well proportion manly development that's even better. A woman's cleavage exposure has been known to open up many opportunities based on her physical, sexual, and enhanced attractiveness. The low necklines of summer and evening wear, gowns with swimwear included has a most seductive, and flirtatious attributes to entice a man's erotic pleasure. Career moves are built on it by tramps and sluts alike, as well as dating the man she is interested in having. The benefits are astronomical in what use to be a fast track to success, and now a day's depending on the woman and the technique she uses. In all walks of life teasing or getting a man's attention a woman's persona handed down from mother to daughters alike all over the world. Which become so eminence that women have gone to great lengths to having breast enlargements with implants to enhance their bodies improvements to get the attention she was not getting in her past. Normal adversity became a thing of the past when the future began with big tits, what made a woman so unique with large breast was the type of women that possesses them in size. So next time you see a woman with large breast with cleavage popping out at you think bon appetit.

Chapter-44

<u>Covering Your Bases</u>

When dating different women know the directions you want to go in before striking up a conversation about getting better acquainted. The best way to start after getting formal hello's out of the way is to start with formal question like how are you doing, and is life treating you well. Then began with what do you like to do for fun, and do you like any games or sports. Ask if she has any hobbies and goals, and if so what would be a good time you could get together to make plans for an exciting weekend. This will give you an idea of the type of woman she is with the type of personality she has. With a long look into her character concerning her mental preferences, without judging her moral philosophy or her decision making about life. Understanding who she is and what she's about will give you more leverage than trying to figure her out. Curious minds only prevail only when you let her thinks she right, even when she's wrong. It may not qualify her as your soul mate but at least you can make an effort, this will give you the insight you need to determining if she is even worth dating. Don't be disappointed if the women you like don't meet up to your expectation. Meaning, if she is not future wife material then continue your search until you find the one that is. When you find her you will know it, there will be a insatiable amount of chemistry between the both of you unimaginably compelling. A force of magnetism so seductive the feelings alone will almost over whelm your emotion with self gratification. You will be hardly able to contain your expression of excitement unimaginatively, unable to put what you feel or have to say into words. Always capitalize on family and structure which lets her known that you are very family oriented. This will make for a good conversation in your discussions when going into the next phase of the dating process. Stay focused on attitude and facial expressions when entering the stages of personality comparison, this will show her a side of you that she can endure, while putting out an all out effort to cover your bases.

Chapter-45

Know What A Woman Wants

Every woman wants a man with financial stability rich or poor as long as he has a job, and in most cases good looks don't hurt. Depending on what's included in your relationship when it comes to helping her pay the bills, endorsed by the evidence of what type of job a man has based on his rate of pay he receives each month or week. This gives a certain appeal to what she see in you as a good provider and a husband to be. This comes without getting the boot which is backed by popular demand while giving her a multitude of plans and ideas in visualizing every aspect on what she wants in her life to be with the man she love. A woman choices set the principles on her belief that she will be with a man financially stable for the rest of her life. No woman want to go through the stages of paying all the bills with no help when the economy has went belly up; times are hard enough as it is with two incomes not to mention just one. This is a necessity any woman in her right mind would want concussive on what a relationship should be, which is team work. Without it your foundation will crumble, no woman wants to be alone, no woman wants to struggle. When the laws of dating have no boundaries you will never make it as a couple, limits brings empty promises leaving facts to hang in the mist. And the only facts that you will see is a long good bye to an exit. In all walks of life opposites do attract, depending on the individuals a man must learn what a woman likes. Build a rapport with your lady because she is the best friend you got, it may not mean much to most but at least you know what she wants, compatibility and sensitivity is located next door to trust.

Chapter-46

If A Woman Is Separated

Men should never date women that's been separated from her ex-boyfriend, for the simple reason that she has not gotten over him completely. Keep in mind if you do get involved with this woman you will retain the hurt she has for her ex, if you get into any kind of altercation about life concerning where you stand in the relationship as a man. It only becomes a bad idea when you hookup with a woman that's been in an abusive past relationship. No matter the situation rather she was the giver or the taker of the abuse, she will only end up very vengeful and vicious. Set off by a combination of past events that will become lethal in the shape of blame, formed to get you caught up in some mess that you will be sorry for later. This is a stipulation incurred into the rules of dating to protect your sanity, if you value your freedom. Always be careful of the traps that's waiting around the corner to happen, by women that's out to do one thing after she has been hurt by men that's did her wrong, seek vengeance. It really don't matter who you are or what you look like, and what you have. In a woman's affliction to harm you in any way of humiliation the validity of violence that she feels has no measure of the pain a man will feel if you get in her way. If the devil comes knocking make damn sure you have a way out, especially if she starts acting stupid and crazy to no end of what a woman's scorn depicts. When a woman becomes argumentative with no intention of listening to reasoning, it become second nature for her to transform into the beast from hell with no understanding based upon the multitude of issues lost into the underbelly of common sense. The mere thought of understanding to her is being in a foreign land lost in the back of her mind from the concept of being hurt. "So there is no understanding".

Chapter-47

How A Woman Thinks

A woman thinks in connection with one chain link after another (hand over fist). If it's in her will of thinking the methods to her madness make sense, by being collectively well organized when it comes to dating with sophistication. Then there's nothing a man can say while trying to explain to her that there is another side to the story in what she see's, far as men and women dating. However she has already made up in her mind when it comes to dating that she has explored every avenue there is to know about certain type of men she is looking for in her adventures of dating. This has already been predetermined in her prediction made up in her mind based on past relationships of her life experiences. This is known as prepense alterations made on purpose of premeditation. The man she chooses has already been chosen knowing in her mind of what she wants, way before she seeks her mate. This is depending on the type of woman she is based upon the attire she wears. Her attractiveness alone has men wishing they were her type of man, which is only reduced to wishful thinking. Certain women are very skillful adversaries when it comes to dating, and going after the man she wants while becoming a well conditioned face of charm.

Chapter-48

When A Man Shares His Woman

When going in and out of a relationships, and you and your girlfriend are not getting along no matter what the case maybe. The logical thing to do is separate, give yourselves enough time and space to reevaluate your differences. Know that during the separation process you or her are not obligated to stop dating or seeing other people. However, if for some reason your girlfriend decides she wants to start seeing other men, the picture becomes clear that she wants to try something new other than the day to day quarrels she had with you. Do she still love you maybe, do she still care it's possible; But whatever the reason rest assure if you love her you will be sharing your woman with other men. There are a number of ways you can look at this, that if she don't find what she is looking for during her escapades of dating, and decide she wants to stay with the fellow she met. You can always have hope that you two will reunite given the thought that she is willing to give you another chance long as your ego don't get the best of you in winning her back. Which will leave you and him trapped between sharing your woman, and she since she feels that it was your fault in the first place. She may feel this is punishment enough in seeing other men that might bring you to your senses in treating her better, just to let you know how much she can make you suffer. She don't necessarily have to be screwing any one, but the game she is playing is to get your attention in order for you to appreciate her more as your mate. This can become a seriatim of events that could start with ignoring you completely.

Chapter-49

If You Just Got Out Of A Relationship

If you been in a relationship for a number of months or years, and you and your ex-girlfriend or wife have split up for good. Give yourself seven months to three years to readjust to the methods of dating; if you don't you will find yourself on a merry-go-round from hell, here's why. The danger in this can go both ways when reentering the lime light of dating, men and women alike on the internet or in the streets are endangering themselves with situation that can cost them their very life. Depending on the type of person you're dealing with during the course of being single while making the necessary adjustments to get over the person you were once involved with. Avoid drama of unwanted conversations or texted messages, when you find someone new that turns out to be coming with the same bullshit you been through before, you'll know by keeping your eyes and ears open. Then again you could forgive your ex-girlfriend, if you and her can come to a understanding and want to patch things up to reconcile your differences, unless you're at the point of no return. The possibilities are endless no matter what the case may be just as long as you give yourself time.

Chapter-50

Illegal Citizens On Sites

Illegal women and men that are on dating sites just find American citizens to legalize there stay here in America, have only one common purpose in mind and that's screwing us over in the process any way they can. They come off sweet and nice but they are not. If you are chatting online with these type of people stop it, because if she is in another country it will cost you a fortune getting her here no matter how sincere your connection of love is, all she wants is to get here and leave you so she can do whatever she can to help her on people. My suggestion to you is forget about it and move on because you are only setting yourself up for a hard fall. If they ask you for money nine times out of ten once she get it, you will never hear from her again. So be smart and delete their ass every time they pop up. If you don't you are falling into a trap of misery and what you have to keep in mind is, the majority of these women are poverty stricken and they will do any and everything it takes to get you to send them money in any way they can. Although friendly conversations never hurt anybody as long as it's distinguished between computer pal and not love. Which I'm not saying that a person can't find love in other countries, I'm just saying be careful when you do. There's a thin line coming and going across barrio plains which holds a lot of grey area's if you're going to visit these places. Intel has it that there are risk and I wouldn't want anyone to be invited to dinner over in a foreign land an end up the main course of the meal.

Mixed Up Women

They do whatever it takes to make a man feel he is no better than what she makes him. She will, she won't, she do, she don't want no man that can't follow her rules; She can, she can't give anything better than what you deserve if it don't begin with her, and love is not an option. We find ourselves in different places when it comes to women that men are dating, trying to get a perspective on just what a woman is looking for in a man. Some women say they want a good man, but the question that's often times over looked is, are you a good woman? They will say yes of course, but that's in her nature to tell a man whatever he wants to hear except for defining how she really is. Men meet women here and there in search of what he wants and likes about the lady he see. She might have other male friends in order to compensate her until she finds the guy she wants. Creating a safe haven for herself when things are not going according to plans if what she has in mind don't turn out to be what she wants. This is known as a backup plan for a verbal cushion or sexual gratification. In my observation don't date women with male friends, for in her mind she feels it's okay to have a serious relationship while having a full blown skeleton in closet at her beck and call, while looking at the size of that bone. This type of woman won't change her image or lifestyle for any man no matter how good he may treat her. This reflection on these type of women are empty without compassion in loving a man for the sake of belonging to no one but herself; and crazy as it may seems, it has become a continuous pattern for a women caught in the mix of a never ending denial. Referenced to view the truth about herself leaving her depressed and all alone.

Chapter-52

Women Thats Been Hurt

Many women have suffered from mental and physical abuse, based on statistic's this has been an ongoing occurrence that has left women battered and bruised. In certain cases depending how long she was in the relationship, most women are able to conveniently bounce back, and live more productive lives. Do to intervention and counseling to counter the effects of their abuse that they have suffered, having these types of programs in place women has a chance at reentering the dating atmosphere once again, however the lingering effects of abuse stay with most women which makes it hard to accept a man's honesty. When he is being genuinely truthful about the way he may feel about her. If she becomes silent or to inquisitive or constantly changes the subjects without letting you finish explaining the first question she ask, then she is pretty much damaged good. If she becomes demanding or argumentative without cause in something you said, or asked her. Then the conflicts of reasoning is pretty much shot, and she may be suffering from E.D.H.D. These are the sure signs of women that are emotionally unstable, and having a solid meaningful relationship with her will always remain out of focus or out of touch, and definitely out the question to date.

Chapter-53

Dating Women
That's Out To Hurt You

Many times in the dating game women are looking to play games with men rather than have a serious relationship. The reason being is due to the facts that they have been hurt themselves, and in many cases a women perception on how she perceives the guy she's dating is pretty much how she will treat them. Rules of engagement (101) has it when a man that's willing to commit, can't always identify the right woman finds himself involved with the wrong one. Unaware that this lady has made a pledge to hurt, and bring much pain as she can towards any man interested in taking a chance with a nut case from hell. This poor tormented reckless creature uses men only to serve her sick demented selfish tendencies, in order to satisfy her own self satisfaction to accommodate her amusement in controlling or hurting a man in any way that she can. Her verbal and abusive behavior characterizes her true feelings towards men by insulting their intelligence as if they don't know what she is doing. By trying to make you think that you're the crazy one with jealousy of threatening malicious intent complete with a language of its own. The humiliation that she causes comes with an open window that plays a key role in the way that she talks to a man in public, around friends if she has any, or family members resulting in gossip that this woman need psychiatric evaluation scheduled for research immediately. My final thoughts concerning this issue, is to disassociate yourself from a woman of her personality fast. Nothing more nothing less.etc . . .

Chapter-54

Women Lie More Than Men

This could be because they lack the confidence to tell the truth and fear of rejection, not saying that all women do depending on the kind of person she is. However it has been proven that women are more clever at lying than men especially when it comes to deceit, discussion, coercion, guilt, composed in the many different assortments of reasons why women feel the need to lie. Women lie about their looks, kids, and the more serious variety of other men. Not to mention the sneaky shit from all the slick shit she did, secrets that hide outside relationships that gives her giggles much laughter. They even lie to tell a lie on top of the lie they told, and the reason is because they feel they will never ever get caught. This has open a lot of men eye's about good women, they lie about their problems from the things she has at works, she lies about the affair she had when she was once fucking her boss. She even lie about how many times she fucked him to protect herself from you thinking that she ain't nothing but a whore. I guess personality plays a role and color don't make a difference; these women are barbaric in nature vicious to the core. A pathological liar being to such a degree that it is to the extreme of being spoiled rotten and conveniently disturbing. These intriguingly fascinating women are not the ones to be dating which make dating that much complicated when men don't have a clue what to look for. A man's only concentration is only interested in one thing a woman's body, they have no concerns about if the women are telling the truth or not. If men capitalize on the facts of the way women are it could make an impact on having a better relationship, with the women that are going to be truthful about having a honest relationship. This will give much added value to words people tend to take for granted, trust. So basically this simple word that has the complexity behind the definition carries a lot of weight when building a solid foundation to a relationship with no lies.

Chapter-55

Don't Date Women In Morn

Dating women that has lost someone close to them rather it was her husband, boyfriend, family member, or best friend; Plays a key role in getting back into the swing of things when living in a society full of the known and unknown obstacles of death. No matter the situation family members are included, giving her the support needed to carry on in a world full of tragedies that could damage a person's self esteem for life. When a man encounters a woman placed in these types of situation and she opens up to you while in transition of getting back onto the dating field. Try to keep an open mind about all she has been through in adapting to someone she lost, by giving her support in the stages of her life as being extremely vulnerable to the expression of words that could be harmful without compassion, if you don't add a delicate touch. Evaluate the facts that this is a woman not to be rushed about anything other than needing your comfort in helping her feel better. Besides you don't want her to start backing away from you if you're just starting to develop feelings for her. Be supportive in all she is doing in whatever stages of transformation needed to build a solid relationship with you. By concentrating on developing communication skills to reconcile any disagreements or differences you might have. This will enhance her love she has for you avoiding any future problems that comes to no end.

Chapter-56

Don't Date
Very Religious Women

It starts with a prayer using "God" as a beacon of light to guide her to the man of her religion. Men that are not that religious dating women of this caliber is not a good idea, maybe to see if there's any compatibility for a one night date. The end results usually remains the same, let life light the way she will say when two worlds are very different, each and everyday she ask "God" for forgiveness while being mean to others just because she's Christian. If a woman entire life is revolved around going to church how she will have time for you or anything else a man likes to do besides going to church. These type of women on these dating sites don't believe in nothing outside of church, far as having fun other than thinking that's it's a part of the devil deceit in bringing a man down. In her mind surrounded with the possibilities of trying to find a husband while making sure he has religion based on her analogy what she feels to be true. Everything she say's and feel God is in her words, could this be from all the hurt she feels smashing into her emotions? Controlling her behavior and moods while reciting scriptures from the Bible; The King James version is what she said was the title. Committed to saving your soul cause she is holier than thou, but will walk right pass you on the streets and won't even speak, while looking right in your face as if you are some kind of freak. They accept all praises because it comes so easy, but not when it comes to dating where accommodations is needed. If you don't go to church or have a bible in your hand then you're not a child of God, I find this to be stupid in saying if not rather odd. Looking at me as if my mind is filled with tar, best wishes to them all as they promote self awareness on religion. I hope she finds the man of her dreams who is upright and very religious, in all of life many complexities from a start that will never finish, with in herself for what it's worth with a search of a new beginning; I hope she has the stamina to go the extra distance. Suicide is not an option if it's base on just conclusions let it be a lesson learned, because God knows what she's doing. Also, if she never find her mate that is separated by time then loneliness cannot be measured based on just religion. When life's unexpectancies leaves you to your own decisions.

Chapter-57

A Womans Scorn

Have you ever had a date that was stern in her confidence with an alluring natural beauty? When somehow you have found yourself giving all you can to keep this woman happy, but what you give her is not enough to please the beast within. While feeling like some poor investor hoping this deal pays off, especially when she's draining you for everything you got, she emptied two years of savings from your only bank account. Now that your money's gone so will she be real soon and all the magic you use to share in and out of Hotels rooms, you wanted your lady to have the best, and champagne was included. After two weeks you told her you loved her and wanted her to be your wife. You spent eighteen hundred dollars for an engagement ring you haven't seen since that night; When you told her about your business plans thriving with ambition, now here comes the arguments about your money that you are spending. In order to get your business off the ground so you can make a decent living, but that's not what she wanted to hear only that you were giving. Now you're just a castaway left with bad intention, wishing you had never met this bitch that left you with mixed emotions, lost without the respect for love because you feel left out. There's nothing like a woman's scorn to keep a man's mind in doubt.

Chapter-58

What Happen to Your Feet

Have you ever had a date where you got to know her intimately; expressing warmth, friendship, love and compassion. While exploring her body sexually from head to toe, with thoughts that would cross your mind like she is part animal or some kind of an aquatic creature cross between a gila monster and crocodile mix. Because by the looks of her feet, they look like she has came right out the woods with toenails as long as a gremlins. Some women feet just need pedicures with treatment that would look better, and some of them need to be cut right off, all the way down to the core. Some women feet you can ignore; if you really think it would help you score, depending on what she looks like in the face, need I say more? So please cover your feet in public ladies, if you haven't given them care, or be the laughing talk of the town like Oprah where everyone will look and stare.

Chapter-59

Have A Strict Don't Tell Rule

Have a strict don't ask don't tell rule when it comes to dating women you don't know. If you have been with other women on dates and it did not work out, this don't need to be discussed in your conversations with your date if you're trying to get to know her. What you did and where you went is really none of her business, if you had a date that ended badly there is no need to volunteer the validity of a situation that went wrong. If you do this will create doubt in the lady you are dating about what she can trust to tell you. Women like confiding in a man she can trust when it comes to expressing her emotions, without the red flags popping up in her mind about the guy she expect you to be with her feelings. Keep your attention on her and the different interests she has in you while making prediction for the future. This will give leverage in making a connection with her on some of the things you have in common. She will evaluate your motives as being genuine while confirming details about the conversations you both was having. As you use this method of thinking in the dating process you will succeed at finding the right woman.

Chapter-60

Don't Date Abusive Guy's

What you see is what you get in every reaction in guy's behavior on how he acts. Men are the number one factors of violence when it comes to physical abuse among women. Based on the contingencies with a cycle of repeating itself no matter the behavior of the man's attitude. It has always played a role in dating Making women much more cautious and careful about the kind man she dates. When she question what she wants and what he says in conversations that will never change the outcome of what it is, now depending on what he does for as his work profession could give her a little more insight into the type of guy she is looking for, depending on the particulars on whom she seek. There is a pattern associated with men that have a distinct behavior in character, which most women can weed out if she is serious about having a meaningful relationship. The benefits of dating can be a lot of fun while taking into consideration that no one wants to be alone, and what makes it all worthwhile is meeting someone for the first time to bring happiness and love a new.

Chapter-61

Emotions Take
Women Day By Day

A woman's mental state of mind comes into play with little or no effort through conscious awareness concerning how she feels, when it comes to dating men with very high standards. In her mind nothing is more important than dating men of quality, these types of men are what makes the dating process all worthwhile. Meaning they know how to treat a lady like a woman when it comes to respect and class upon the highest level of sophistication; Rather it's work or fun you can rest a sure a gentlemen will always be on time, if he is not a man of this caliber, and is not fulfilling his obligation to her as being her lover. Then verbal confrontation could be damaging to the relationship when he is not giving her what she needs. Her composure of status shows her appreciation when the man is being supportive of her needs. A woman's mental state plays a huge role in a relationship because she is full of emotions, some are very complex depending on the stages and events surrounding the involvement of the man she is dating. This is a period of experience based on the qualification having psychological understanding through a woman's eye.

Chapter-62

Women That Don't
Want To Be Controlled

It all starts with truth on why she doesn't want to be controlled. It ranges from the past relationship with men rules and regulations on life how a woman should be treating a man. Most women simply want to do whatever they want with no questions asked, women that don't have no respect for men feel that if the man is not paying her bills or putting a ring on her finger has no say so about anything she do. Regardless how a man may feel when they are dating, no wonder there are so many single women. Women are quick to assume the worst about a man if he believes a woman should listen to him when she is asked to do something that will benefit them both. This has become more benevolent through personal differences based on his or her actions. Characterized by her actions expressing how she really feels when it comes to being asked or told what to do, no wonder women are so lonely. Women ego's get the best of them when their mind set is froze with the thought of never letting a man tell them what to do. By this being one of the common factors in a relationship to unsubmissive women that has careers will not submit to men that have control. He doesn't want her telling him what to do because of his leading social status, and she is tired of being told what to do because of her status of being a woman. Both are entertained by destination of power who's only passion is to themselves, and on many occasion women make the rules securing the possibilities on her profile as that unrestrained mass of flesh standing politically correct. This is a woman without a road paved in gold. These are women with a history of bad apples and dirty deeds towards men experiencing the freedom of being in control. Now that he is dating, women of this nature tend to be very complicated and hard to manage because of her outlook on men. The reasons being is because she is scared, afraid of commitment of being tied down because of the one thing she loves and needs most, (control). As long as a woman can manipulate a man into what she wants she will skillfully get all she can from a man without any strings attached. Pathetic as it may seem for her there is no turning back; these are the terms of endearment conditions of a lost soul. Women of this nature are meant to be alone when they don't want to be controlled.

Chapter-63

Dating Women
In Other Countries

Dating women in faraway places has more holes in a wall and down falls than ups and downs. Fate has it unless you've met a person from another country and you both decide to stay in touch, up on them returning to the place they are from. Then you just might be shit out of luck, for the simple reason if you're trying to build a long term relationship, depending on his or her character and the type of person they are it could be a waste of your time. In every long distance relationship if it doesn't cross your mind or maybe in the back of your mind that he or she could be seeing someone else. If it's a woman depending on the circumstances of her living condition, it's quite possible that she might be a prostitute providing sexual services to compensate her way of living. These are one of many branches of dating women from other countries may have, or if it is a man he could be a pimp, playa or even a gigolo offering sex indiscriminately for his own sole purpose of getting paid. Not to mention the risk of health factors that plays a key role in getting to know someone. You cannot look at a person's picture over the internet and determining rather their healthy or not; There is no way you can see the symptoms on what a person may or might not have or tell the condition of their health mentally or psychically if they are sexually active. Unless you have trusted medical doctor's analysis on a person's medical information you cannot be sure of the outcome. I'm not saying what a person may or might not have, all I'm saying is be very careful when dating people from other parts of the world for the life that you save . . . just might be your own.

Chapter-64

Dazed And Confused

Men and women dating should have a protocol that when you meet someone over the internet and they don't look nothing like the picture they posted when you see them. You should be able to immediately excuse them from your presence if they don't look nothing like what they said, if you speak to them over the phone and they describe to you their lifestyle and you agree that he or she is someone that you want to be with or possibly meet. Then there shouldn't be any speculation of the person you're going to see; However sometimes that's not always the case, If he or she is dressed as if they came right out of a comic book or drug rehab, that should be grounds enough without any further conversation to walk right pass them. Giving the nature on what their intentions maybe if they seem animated in character which appears to be very different from what they were over the phone, gives you the right to follow protocol. For example I had several conversations with women by comparison discussing what they wanted out of a relationship if I was their man. They replied that they did not want a relationship only a friend, and they were not looking for marriage or anything of the sort. So I asked them what is the purpose of you being on a dating site if you're not serious; these are some of the main reasons women get treated like shit because of women like this that's only out to play games. So when a lady that's genuinely serious about having a relationship with some guy that she is interested in. She end up getting a raw deal from a guy that's out to get back at women because of something that was done to him by some slut. You try to make sense of it all by excusing the ignorance of the women with the problems, because these basket cases don't have a clue, who they are, what they're doing or where they're going. Unaware of the facts about the surrounding consequences behind their reckless behavior of being stupid. I would never want to meet a woman so dumb ever again, who's conversation is more of gibberish followed by the sounds of yadda yadda yadda which leaves me with the thoughts of being . . . somewhere in the twilight zone. In my closing statement it has become imperative to flood the minds of the people that don't know the reasons concerning inexperienced women, and their lack of knowledge on what to say when involved with men on these websites. It has become conclusive that these women need to be taught how to respond to positive behavior when a man is being genuinely open and honest to her needs. This will give them guidance in developing their communication skills in channeling a better method of thinking, when dating men of virtue.

Chapter-65

Pointing Out His
Or Her Short Comings

Imperfection is part of human beings genetic make up; it is a quality no one want to endure. We look to one another to give ourselves popularity for who we are in becoming more of what we want, by accepting what we see from the eye's of people that see you as being perfect. Which no one is perfect at all; It don't matter how good you look we all have flaws with conditions. Some with bumps, scars, piercings or tattoos in exchanging the look of imperfection. You could be the ugliest person in the world base on looks alone that could be the most perfect person of them all; with a beauty inside and out. Displaying a wonderful mind and a soul that endures all ridicule, because critics know nothing when it comes to fate that stands the test of time. Which is not a misfortune at all, because beauty is only skin deep and knowledge has no flaws. So never judge a person on the way they look just accept them for who they are. Because you never know if you may need that person when a bad situation occurs; they might be the only one around at the time in that moment when you need help the most. Because one day you might just find yourself rejected from friends acceptance, rejection is just a small price to pay when you refuse to show reluctance. So if we reframe from the negative thoughts on who's better or greater than most, we just might find peace of mind and bypass our negative suffering.

Chapter-66

When You're Not Compatible

Compatible is being capable of existing together in harmony freely expressing the way you feel about a person. The ideology of this concept applies when two people are dating and have absolutely nothing in common except for the fact of the way they look. True to the facts that opposites do attract even if you have nothing more than conversation, but if he or she don't like anything other than fucking without the experience of sharing and doing things together; Then the relationship isn't going to last if a man likes running the streets and hanging out with his buddies and never spend time with his lady. It's just a matter of time before she looks for someone else to give her the time that she needs. Women love attention and having fun with a man that gives her lots of it, ranging from movies to shopping and taking long walks in the park as your watching the stars at night. All of this is important in a relationship so you don't grow apart; you both have to agree with what will work to keep the two of you happy. This comes without displaying a manipulative behavior based on ones attitude on who's right and who's wrong. As a couple you must accept each other for who you are and judge yourselves for what you're not, whether you have something in common to share contrary to what you like most about the person you are dating. This is a combination that will leave you with the thought of being appreciated, with the respect of treating the person you're dating like the woman or man you want them to be. However, if you do come across that jerk who's appearance is associated with the dissatisfaction in the nature of his character as being a manifestation of his multiple personalities consistent with his elements or surroundings. Distance yourself from this type of guy's very quickly, for they are the epitome of turmoil without any compassion other than to service no one needs but their own.

Chapter-67

Change Of Ideas

Don't be the man with a lot of emotion when it comes to romance by trying to be creative in coming up with the right thing to say, go with the flow of the conversation when there are questions asked by responding as quickly as possible. Try to be as comforting as possible by giving her a sense of security, women love being in the presence of a man where she feels safe. Rather you're dating for fun, or romance into having a serious relationship. Make any type of changes you need in order to have a good time with the person you're dating. She may not have a babysitter, or he is having problems with his car; Whatever the case maybe always try to have a back-up plan if you can, no matter what occurs. It's also important to remember that if you have never met this person before other than talking to them over phone, always let someone know where you are each and every time you meet. Our lives is an open book with certain patterns when responding to the people we meet, and in doing so . . . we must understand and prepare ourselves for every out come when we can; although it may not be a normal one. It is an endless process when dating that allows us to find the person we like, as well as the ones to avoid. This method helps keep us safe when responding to messages over the internet while keeping an open mind into the many dangers of the predators that lurk about.

When avoiding people reacting to the negative responses of behavior, when we come into contact with someone you don't know. No matter how you live your life when exploring the many avenues of change, always remain vigilant with people that you don't know online.

Chapter-68

Difference In Matter Of Opinion

It doesn't matter if it's a friend, family member, work, or church members. Disagreements happens all the time with each person that is viewing it differently, for instance if you're dating someone that use to date your friend or a family member, men and women alike, but this is mostly directed at women. If there was no connection depending how long they dated then there shouldn't be a problem with you dating her if you have a connection. Rather it be mental or a physical attraction then there shouldn't be an issue about the two of you being together, especially if there are deep displayed signs of affection. However, if she or he have dated a friend or family member six months to a year, well that can be an issue concerning his or her better judgment. Just because it didn't work out with them doesn't mean it will be okay for you to date this man because your sista or cousin don't want him. That would be sick and demented in every aspect of low class perfidy. When dealing with such disrespect there are a number of things to consider if you find yourself faced with this kind of dilemma. 1) How long have you known this person? 2) What was you and her relationship before you two got together? 3) Were there any kind of chemistry between the two you before you got together? 4) Have she ever called or texted you on any occasion concerning problem or issues she had with your friend or family member? These are the question to answers that require the analysis of research before you consider getting involved with a person that has been with a friend or family member coming abroad. The outcome of these types of situation are more negative than positive in expressing love with someone you know, but never knew their feelings until the moment opinions never mattered until you got together to find the truth.

Chapter-69

Men Have Feelings Too

It has been exaggerated that men are oblivious toward women feelings. This is a stereotypical fabrication of truth that has been the topic where every relationship has gone bad. I've been in, and seen enough relationships to know, that this isn't always the case. In many situation involving a woman's overly obsessive behavior when she is feeling emotionally disturbed. They want men to think that we are insensitive toward their needs or wants when they can't get what they need; also it is said men don't listen to women when communicating in discussion about her decision when they disagree. If a woman can't coax a man into seeing things her way, then she feels you lack the compassion or knowledge on providing her the support she needs to fulfill her demands at the time of having things go in the direction of the way she want you to be. Acting as if there's some type of chronological methods in what she say or do; you will not understand at the time of her expressing what she feels is right. This has been a process pertaining to a woman's emotion by not taking in account how a man might feel when it comes to expression his emotions on subjects leading the majority of the time to arguments; destroying the very fabric of order in a relationship that has no meaning when two people can't resolve issues on what each person might feel. Until men and women resolve these types of problems there will always be question and answers followed by the thoughts that men have feelings too.

Chapter-70

Dating Women That's Curious

Women that have infidelity relationships are into having more than one partner; rather it's a man or woman having a social behavior of most animals. Will always be the lowest form of the human race wanting nothing more, but to spread their sexual exploits with a never ending lust in their addiction to satisfy an uncontrollable sexual gratification. This combination comes with the entertainment rating to do nothing more than fuck. These kind of people are nothing more than freaks of nature pleasing at random younger viewers with a mature content bringing them into their world of deceit; With no filter under the common laws of the government to allow explicit adult behavior which is now at a click of a button. This intense unrestrained sexual craving for lust over whelming as it may seem, is a desire manifested. When two people in a relationship are not satisfied with the person they are with or want something more than a serious relationship when a relationship becomes too serious. Some of these sluts that are bisexual women . . . whom have relationships with men, when the women that they are seeing is not taming the beast within to reach climax often times takes much more than a stiff tongue; are these women and men bi-curious no. Either you are or you're not. When it comes to being what you are there is no being guilty for women when being attracted to men they like. Their sexual orientation is pretty much cut and dry when it comes to their enthusiasm that reflects the outcome of who they are. What you need to know is . . . when you're engaging in this kind of social behavior you are exposing yourself to the many different types of diseases to ease their illicit sexual appetites, causing the body harm which impairs the normal functions of the body organisms. In most cases depending on what you have can be cured, in others like H.I.V . . . or Aids, you will find only death.(Diagnosis) . . . Which in over all cases it's likely to be H.I.V that's unrelenting; there is nothing normal about being bisexual, homosexual, lesbian, or gay. Oh sorry, I said that already. However, we live in a world that has no boundaries into the demonic urges of a thriving community of the sick and demented (misfits). Now that I just set it off to let those of you who don't know, that they are all going to burn in hell, which is a link between alternate lifestyles frequently expressing their perspective while constantly holding their breath from all the shit that's about get blown sky high. So there will be no confusion for those of you that get freaked out and scared in case you decide to change from that lifestyle or burn for all of eternity beneath hell.

Chapter-71

Dating Controlling Women

In my analysis through extensive research; I have learned that when men are dating most women that's financially stable. They tend to be overly bearing if not quick to judge harshly with a mindset of a very controlling nature. With a defensive mannerism when speaking to you is more like talking at you then talking to you, which has became a distinctive trait of speech of hers that's become more annoying than anticipated by the men she's looking to date. Creating an act of her state of being that seems to be it's either her way or no way at all. This quickly pushes men away from their enormous attitudes that speaks help . . . because she has not yet learned how to express herself to be desired other than being rigid in nature with a very high self esteem, with expectation which offsets her style entirely when she is not getting her way; or getting what she wants from the men she dates. This has become an issue when men have become victims by controlling women that minds seem to be more isolated and confused because they are dealing with much deeper issues from complexities within themselves. Now that there is evidence based on their never ending quest to find a meaningful relationship, it is not common that they will never confess to having a problem for the simple reasons of losing control. Most men don't allow women of this caliber to control them for fear of making them feel weak and insignificant. A man of statue will not put up with this period. Most of these women exercise emotional and verbal control where she will become a lesbian in order to get better resorts from her same sex counterpart making the man obsolete to her demands of control. Which has became a parody of ridicule held in the folds of Americans diagnosis and disorder. Making it so that the man is not the issue here, but the women are. When it comes down to who's wrong and who's right it turn into a scary movie of same sex relationships and homosexuality remains in control.

Chapter-72

Dating Controlling Men

Let me start by explaining the psychological aspects of the controlling man to gain a much clearer view into the behavior of his methods of thinking. Which involves his dominating attributes when calling the shot in a relationship while dating. These type of men are selfish in nature and narcissists out to prove their dominance used to denote a woman by expressing who he is. Not realizing his imperfections of elitism to women has become a plight of indifferences do to his belief that he should rule without compassion. Dark as it is to find a solution that's only been around since the caveman days, their personalities with mind set are very egotistical. Which is a trait ordinarily found in the majority of men being fascinated with one self deriving from his own excessive admirations. This is a psychological conditioning of the mind that characterizes his lack of compassion without understanding a woman's situation or feelings; limiting his motives toward his fixation in controlling what he cannot see. The only way to bring order in these type of men is through serious counseling, when their minds are limited to logic or understanding based on his lack of common sense. This is based on his inappropriate behavior towards women when his idea of having a good time is knocking her upside the head while being so rudely arrogant into thinking is right because he is man.

Chapter-73

Women That
Like Being In Control

She moves like the flow of an exotic stream, her gown in harmony with strides screaming pure ecstasy draped in a silhouette against the curves of her body. Outlined in a fashion that words can only begin to describe with an appearance of sheer clean while promoting her habits of excellent condition of health easy to be seen. She is never uncertain of herself, but sometimes lost in thought. Planning on what she will do next cause she has a date tonight. The information that men gives her is how she determines who is right. Women of this caliber is on every mans waiting list, some of them with fantasies of her being their trophy wife. A woman's over all conviction is controlling what she wants and see's one day at a time sets her position boosting her ego when men respects her role as a independent woman. While controlling the advancements from men that promises her everything with no restriction in rank for what he offers as being a man. Her knowledge is the key ingredient of love she has for others which signifies her well being as a woman with compassion that lights the way for women in scorn.

Chapter-74

Don't Date Men
That's Been With Other Men

Men that's been with other men has the highest transmitted disease rate among the human population in the world. The risk of infection is apparent there is no denying you getting infected; there is no prevention because it's wrong. This is the lowest forms of human beings on the face of this planet no matter how they try to clean it up or slice it. This is very nasty and disgusting for people to even think that it has a place in society humanitarian establishments. It is offensive, physically immoral without such a taste to go so far as to say that this is as vast as space related to forms unknown. The theological aspects of the indifferences dates way back since biblical days, based upon the nature and the will of God revealing that men with men will not be tolerated since Sodom and Gomorrah. This was so severely punished and lead to the overall destruction to gays, punks, fagots as we know them. This is much worse than being a dog like animal and the psychological complexities over ruled by peoples analogy. When in today's society everyone seems to be more concerned about freedom of expression, when expression is harming the very fabric of our society. Not to mention how homosexuality is becoming more confusing for our youth as if not to know if they should be male or female, while dealing with what they see than the actual facts of who and what they are. This is a transition they should not dispute when knowing what they are as a person when it comes to their gender. Our days are surely numbered if people think they can continue on lending a blind eye to something so prevalent that has become so widespread barreling into the souls of Christians, as they juggle with fate of sin on the twisted wind. While trying to convince themselves that it is okay for these people to be living a lie.

Chapter-75

When Dating Certain Women

Depending on what you're looking for that makes your search unique, when trying to find the lady that you want and like. Rather she's tall, skinny, fat, and stout, that comes in the many shapes and forms women come in. Even smaller than a midget below the average norm; women have certain personalities which links them to their looks of indifferences. That gives each one a certain appeal of status tapping into what she likes in a man when revealing some of her secrets. Catching some of these women is like an art of class supported by a style all of her own, you can be confident in your approach while expressing your interest in what you see. However, unless she gives you notice you will be basically wasting your time, what gets women attention is looks and personality of the way a man carries his self. If you come at her like some untrained pet, that's exactly how she will treat you, like the animal you are. There are many techniques and strategies men can use that often times seem to work without making them seem desperate or in need of help. The one I've seen that works the best is the one that starts with hello, while having an insatiable magnitude of charm followed by a quaint peculiar style opposed to melt her doubts away. Once you see that light of her smile on her face her heart will open for love, giving you the chance to set the date for a life time of true romance. Now I'm not saying this works with every man with the female species, because every woman is different. It may not work with some at all, but give or take a few. I can assure you if you talk to enough women the odds will be in your favor. If you take your time in trying to find that single and special lady just keep your cool while staying smooth because it's all in the matter of process.

Chapter-76

Don't Leave Long Messages To Women Online

When dating women online and the man is interested in meeting the woman of his choice; He will leave her a message expressing that he would like to know her better and if she is interested she will respond. However some men take it too far by leaving long drawn out stories about his interest in the woman that he is pursuing, clearly over powering the expression he intended. Which sends up red flags to women because it seems this guy is desperate and may not have her best interest at heart. In my advice to men don't leave long messages to women, keep it short and to the point purely expressing your interest in what you like about her profile and the way it makes you feel. Then wait for her response in hopes that she is the one in making your dream come true. Women are very skeptical when it comes to online dating because of the many different types of social predators online. There have been so many reported negative stories about men and women dating online from rape, stalking, murder, robbery, identity thief and much much more. To the extent that women have to be careful more so than men, because of their vulnerability to fall prey. This has become a weakness in the computer system that can result in harm to the systems operation or the people that question it's safety, when exploited by hostile people that's looking to cause you physical or emotional harm. That's why men must be careful and take the precautions when expressing themselves when making any kind of advances toward the women they meet. Always let the lady give the indication how, where, and when, they would like to meet so there will be no misunderstanding about your intentions on getting to know her. Make sure she's comfortable with you in every way in making contact concerning your action towards a man she never met. So remember in the back of her mind you are still a stranger.

Chapter-77

Date With Confidence

In many cases when men are dating have a tendency to lose confidence in themselves when approaching women that their interested in meeting. In my analysis on the subject that goes into the various details on how to overcome these issues. Lets our minds explore the many options that are available when channeling your thoughts of the lady you have in mind. Which helps men to overcome his problems that keeps him from pursuing the woman wants. The main reason most men have these issues is they don't know how to shed their insecurities that's linked to their behavioral patterns of guilt, lacking the confidence on what other people might say or think. Depending on what his position or status is and whom he is associated with; keeps them in the dark on how he should go about expressing his interest without feeling like a fool. Let's start by opening a few doors to building morals and having an understanding to your character preferences, by resetting your mind to the women that's most likely to fit your life style on the way that you live. If you're business oriented you might want a woman long term in a relationship as a business partner to ensure that your finances will always remain in order once you two have establish trust with each other. This will define her likes and dislikes as well as yours, triggering love in the simplest form. To a degree where you both can advance into a meaningful relationship once you both have established that you are working for the same goal, and that is called peace of mind. What men tend to over look are the possibilities which goes beyond meaningless conversation or laughter in trying to make a connection that shouldn't be connected in the first place. The art of dating is nothing like a game of chance when you're dealing with human emotions. This is not a variation of artificial intelligence when approaching women with ambition for a singles dream of finding someone to fall in love with. The complexities of the human heart and soul that it is God's will that every man should have somebody to love.

Chapter-78

Playing The Mind Game

Inside and out outside looking in, thinking how to get what you want is when the game actually begins. Short term or long term the search can be empowering with psychological principles to all that dare to ask. A very optimal experience where all the rules apply, depending on what your methods are in finding someone to meet. In the dating game the rules always change depending on who you meet, with a look or a stare like truth or dare you're taking a chance with cheats. Experiments specials reveal mental tricks in relationships that you hope will last, with phrases or words that represents love where you might suffer your losses. The energy you put into it will be a game well played at best; where temperatures boils from women and men because somebody feelings were hurt. The objective here is to follow protocol, but is it all just stuck in our minds . . . searching for love while embracing the game when your mind is filled with so many options. How can you choose when there are so many choices, and your versions of the lies are mixed with the truth; dazed and confused that keeps us amuse of our frenzy for social gathering. In all the events that leaves our heart in content while playing with online dating. The more we gravitate toward such joyful pain our treachery becomes tears of laughter, with moderate exposure to bring people closer with personalities half insane, with a mental state of mind twisted, but defined with fingertips pressing on buttons; on keyboards that keeps responding to messages left. Which has become somewhat very compelling deep in this mess while full of confessions the facts have already been seen, in what we created the game has been stated that loneliness is not a dream; just one big step from a graveyard away from what our lives will actually be.

Chapter-79

The Short Comings Of Loneliness

Nothing worth having is easy to hold when you have given all that you can, for the love that you had is just another lost soul buried in memories that last. We search our minds remembering good times to comfort our hearts with joy, from the pain that you felt from the love that you left; where your companion has turned real sad. Now you have grief from the fear that you feel, because dating her will be no more. Most of us get a second chance at romance when dating gives you a way in, but don't hold your breath when the lady you meet has rules with certain conditions, just put aside your foolish pride for your love is in need of assistance. Then try to mend your broken heart from a misfortune that has left you empty inside and stop blaming others for what's in your mind; based of your past experiences. Take time out to clear your thoughts away from family and friends, cause loneliness is a unpleasant feeling when you don't get along with others. Surrounding yourself in a empty space trapped in a world of pain.

Chapter-80

The Power Of Words

It is imperative when men are out dating that you choose your words carefully, women are very easily offended if you speak to them in the wrong tone or manner. Words can have an effect upon the way a date is going to go from beginning to end, it will change the way a woman looks at a man instantly. Poorly spoken and poor choice of words bares an impact when you meet your date for the first time, never say anything stupid by asking if she is dating other guy's. She will look at that as an insecurity you have based on your low self esteem, and any chemistry she once had for you is destroyed. This will have her thinking of a way to end the date very quickly by saying she is not feeling well or she has a head ache. These are some of the mistakes men make when trying to make an impression on a first date, if you are uncertain about what to say after introducing yourself. Try complimenting her on the clothes she wears or the smell of perfume she wears, as well as the style of hair. This will ensure the way she will look, and feel about you as long as your style promotes your class. When taking your date out to lunch or dinner always ask what kind of food she likes to eat, and do she like seafood or pasta. Ask which is her favorites and if she is allergic to any fruits or vegetables, this will let her see the caring side of you in establishing concerns for others. The words you speak have incredible power as long as you use them wisely; the surrounding effects impact the truth when held in high expectation. Offering hope to women you don't know in order to connect with caution, to a woman that listen with love on her heart to a man that lead by example.

Chapter-81

Dating In Both Direction

It is a fact that we can only be in one place at one time, only in theory scientist are researching how a person can be in two places at once. Now that people have computers with webcams we can now go in any direction of travel by our image on the screen of our computers, into a multiversity developmental and discretional view by seeing people, places or things on our (PC). We have made that leap through technology in being in many places at one time, physically seen and heard in appearance but not actually there. To take you even further into people's exploration of facts, modern operations has it where men are turning into women and women turning into men: Abomination all over the place. In my further analysis the human race has become more and more confusing than ever, making it almost next to impossible to distinguish the difference between men taking on the form of women. Having sex changes with hormone shots that will never make them a woman, without the organs (God) has intended to be inside a man, men cannot possess the actual feelings of what they are not, a women. They're still men forever trying to be something what he is not. Having memories only in what he sees while denying the very fact of what he is . . . a man, these types of people are in constant denial and have a sickness in nature while being very deceptive. "It must be one of the biggest upsets in the world that they cannot produce a baby." Like a real woman can in every aspect of being a mother. I find it almost suffocating with the thought of having the slightest possibility of being with a transsexual with all the looks of a woman; if I didn't know he was a man. Society has allowed these people to think that it's okay to act and be something he or she is not based on their social origin. This appears to be one of the trends of evolution of the lowest form, while studying the outcome of human nature homosexuality identities. This is not based on facts, but the theories on how people become homosexuals. Disgusting as it is telling people that it is okay to be with the same sex is condemning yourself to hell while claiming to be Christian, praying to the devil himself expecting to be saved by the very creature that wants to see you die. The internet has created even more challenges than ever with all the diversities of a complex mind of everyone sick desires. Expressing thoroughly that dating is not made to be simple, but placed in a bag full of tricks without looking inside to find what you will get, only to find questions to answers with no end.

Chapter-82

Sick And Psychotic Dates

The condition of the mind is often described in many unique patterns and forms. The diagnosis is sometimes characterized by a person's behavior or symptoms, people often times suffer from mental break downs while losing touch with reality. By being in the state of mind of pretending to be someone they're not in order to get next to someone that they want. A lot of women and men have these symptoms of being something or someone they're not, confusing facts with fiction of their mental addiction of trying to be more than what they are. Ranging from hallucination or delusions based on childhood past experiences depending on the abuse they suffered and the medication taken. Also depending on how severe their abuse was at the time of their altercation; giving the indication of abuse is always there from childhood all the way to adulthood. In most cases through counseling, medication, and getting the necessary treatment in order to function in a more stable environment other than the institution that person is use to. Normally they would be able to handle the complexities of main stream America, and the different personalities that interact with social gatherings. Nowadays a woman's main concern is can a man be trusted when they meet without her feeling emotionally detached from signs he displays;

because his personality has changed from the way he was expressing himself over the phone or in texted messages. My suggestion to women is to take the necessary precautions to protect yourself and don't forget the mace.

Chapter-83

Bad behavior Patterns

Having bad behavioral patterns while dating can hinder you from making a love connection with a woman you find compatible to you. This also can change the outlook about the way a woman might feel about you, depending on the way you present yourself. Meaning you doesn't pick your nose, grab your crotch, or belch out loud in public. Which can be very annoying to women to no end; saturating any good thoughts she may have had about you based on your appearance. Men should always conduct themselves as gentlemen when ever going on dates and being in the public eye, being polite and forthcoming gives rapport to your character in establishing the type of person that you are. Always adhere to protocol when taking your date out to eat by going to the restroom to wash your hands before the meals arrive. This will ensure the possibilities of her going on a second date with you in reference to your well behaved manners and cleanliness. In the future always challenge your disciplinary methods when dating women of statue in order to become more successful in finding the one that you want.

Chapter-84

Rude And Obnoxious Dates

Rudeness can be one of the biggest turnoffs in the dating circle, like a child should be so bold by doing stupid things to get attention from their mother. A grown man sometimes act the same way too; for a lot of reasons most men that hasn't matured completely have a tendency to be very obnoxious and selfish by being rude, when they first meet their date; By talking over them or not letting her finish a sentence while she is trying to explain her short coming for being single for a long time. What men have to realize if they listen they just might learn something about the person they are with. To better understand where she is coming from, unfortunately there are those type of men that don't take women very seriously, and take it upon themselves to be entertaining by cracking jokes, or trying to be funny for whatever reason to amuse themselves. Not realizing how silly and immature it makes them look, and the lady that's in his presence resents meeting him because of his character. While putting her in a position of uneasiness and discomfort. Which will now lead to her leaving you because of your action, men must do a better job at considering a ladies feelings when it comes to meeting her for the first time. We pride ourselves on who we are never stopping to think that the way you treat a person defines your personalities or character. Also men have to remember that there's a time and a place for everything as long as things are put in the right perspective, which by comparison when you're dealing with women's emotions there's a fine line that should not be crossed.

Chapter-85

Knowing When
To Leave Your Date

In many situation males and females find themselves attracted to each other over the internet on dating sites all over the world. Sometime if they make a connection while getting to know each other, they feel they're compatible enough to meet. After talking for months, and hours on the phone you both decide to get together. Everything was fine when you were living in separate places until you decide to move together, and as usual you decided to move in with her. Now that you have settle into her home, and find that you're not compatible she wants you to leave. For whatever the indifferences you both had it was determined that you were no longer compatible. We are always curious how long a relationship will last whenever we fall in love, not realizing that it takes time in getting to know the person before you move in with them right away. In order to avoid future drama make sure you get to know a person at least a year before you move in with them. This will give you a chance to analyze their method of thinking before making a wrong decision or commitment that might leave you high and dry. Although no one wants to be single for the rest of their life, peace of mind is the best medicine until you find the person compatible to the way you live.

Chapter-86

A Calculated Misfortune

The ultimate source of lifestyles relating to women and men, at times seems funny how they meet in the beginning rather it's in passing while shopping or just hanging out at the beach or club. Only to discover later that they have nothing in common, sometime we can't help but wonder why they end up getting together in the first place, (just tragic). However from the start of the relationship you did end up with the guy you thought would be the one, and now you're trying to figure out what went wrong. It becomes a bitch when you start dating outside your race when the guy you fell in love with likes little boys or other men. Regina King set sparks when it became very controversial about black women dating other races of men, but what she don't understand is; there's not a man on this planet that can fuck the way a black man can. This can be equally justified by saying the majority of other races of women want to fuck black men, but don't want anything to do with having a child by one unless he's making millions of dollars. In my observation I found that brings facts to light, that a lot of women from other races love being with white men only because they have all the money, as soon as his back is turned they're slinging pussy from east to west to whatever man she desire. Maybe the reasons being she's from a different race, and chooses to be selective no matter the color, region, or religion as long as love is there men will always care for women very deeply.

Chapter-87

What Went Wrong In Her

Mixed emotion comes with many aspects of a relationship, when the man or woman you adore don't turn out to be the one you want to be with. In most cases some problems become so deeply rooted at the end of a relationship that situation can turn real bad very fast. When the ugly arguments occurs and the man becomes abusive it is a fact that the woman will need therapy, to help her cope from suffering a nervous breakdown during the course of her rehabilitation. Most women suffer from bipolar disorder or some form of schizophrenia do to psychological abuse, and some are just plain crazy waiting to hurt men too. I can't help but wonder how much of these women treatment programs really help, a man can often time tell when something isn't right with a woman just by looking in her face. No matter how she tries to hide it, her expression of pain of what she has been through is always there. A woman's mind is never completely stable in life woes from her ups and downs, which make women turn very cold for being friend to foe, never really given a man a chance when he's out to gain her trust. This will take years of healing for women that's been abused by men, bypassing all relationships to find the answer in her soul. Slowly descending on a cloud looking for the answers that comes in a prayer; because dating is not a option when loneliness brings you peace. By putting distance between the hurt she felt from a pass that ran out of love. This is to the bitterness that we call fate with memories left behind.

Chapter-88

Emotional Decision Daters

Emotions plays a key role in everyday life which is essential to our way of living. It becomes a philosophical point of view, as we try to put things in perspective in our lives for the sake of being safe. Our reasons being when it comes to dating is making the right decision in choosing the right type person to date, without setting ourselves up for a fall before becoming too emotionally involved with the person we are interested in being with. By making these types of choices and have the freedom to pick and choose at will. I often times wonder, why is it when everything starts out so great often times end so badly, and my conclusion on this is nobody wants to give the other person the benefit of the doubt any more. It would seem that people have become more dysfunctional than ever; that if the person you meet don't agree with his or her point of views in their methods of thinking. Then you are not deemed worthy of their companionship because of the way they feel, which don't necessarily make it right since people have a right to their own opinions. Clearly there are some issues here that wouldn't make any difference if we learned to accept each other for who we are without making it an issue out of things that bares no significance to the relationship itself. Sometimes we must bend the rules a little just to see if you're right, and what I mean by this is if your date tells you no to a request that you were hoping for a yes; that don't mean that they might not agree to it later. Having understanding lets your date know that you are flexible to their point of views and their decisions. This gives you the leverage needed in gaining trust with your date in developing a meaningful relationship no matter the circumstances or differences you both may have. So keep an open mind about how you feel about certain subjects in a debate when your date might see it another way, and don't be that man or woman that have to have everything their way in order to prove a point about who you are. This just might cause you to lose someone that could be made special in your life all because you have become too emotional.

Chapter-89

Dream Dates

Every date is supposed to start with romance giving the idea a chance to spice up your love life. If you're looking for the ultimate woman while dating rather she a model, musician, actress, or a woman with a government job. Then you would want to explore the anonymous nature of the internet. This will give you a different view of what you're looking for when updating your status base on your life style, but remember that all that shines is not a pot of gold. It can be unsafe in many ways of your search when running into the gold diggers in the industry looking for guys just like you. Trying to sell you a pipe dream about all the things she can and will do for you, and like jewelry in stores all over the world everything comes at a very expensive price. These are very difficult times we live in and every breath we take is precious, there are too many people being setup by men and women alike, and if you're not too careful it just might cost you your life. The majority of people in this world are definitely on the take, so be careful of the one you seek waiting to be discovered.

Chapter-90

An Open Door Inside Dating

Bumps and bruises sometimes leave scars caused by the never ending consequences of dating. The scars, bumps and bruises don't necessarily come by someone putting their hands on you, but the ones that can mentally wear you down. This can be a laboratory of mess gravitating towards the obvious reasons a person stays single. People are avid listeners when it comes paying attention on the latest news in our neighborhoods, and things happening around the world. Like when we search for a particular kind of person when dating, ranging from music to adventure, entertainment, and much much more; Our destiny is powered by the compassion we have for other as well as our own lives. Some people date for the sheer amusement in the pursuit for happiness, while others take a more serious approach when dating as long as it leads to an open door to marriage. The internet gives people a inside look into men and women relationships with all the adversities life has to offer. Sure there's a lot of negative things, but there's a lot of positive into bringing about change in the way you date and how. Which gives us a way we can pick and choose what we like and dislike without facing anyone or thing that we don't want. The option is yours with a menu of chemistry that holds value to a necessity where people are confident with their personality and the person they meet.

Giving a certain amount exposure to who they may or might not be, randomly offering a endless flow of singles, married, or separated men and women a open door inside dating whose sole purpose is to find someone new.

Chapter-91

Close Your Minds Door To No

When you approach a woman and you're thinking in your mind what if she says no, rather you're walking down the street or at a dance club, work, or just simply working out at the gym. Then you open your mind up for rejection as it becomes a condition of the mind. Once you stop entertaining that though you will succeed in your advances when you approach the women you're looking to date. You must be ready to have the idea that all women will say yes, without having doubts or insecurities. Always perceive yourself as being a king of great importance when making your presence to women known, rendering them helpless to everything you ask. We live in a world where women see men as weak, and if you don't stand up for your manhood they will treat you accordingly during the process of your date. All men have to do is follow the signs of a woman's behavior patterns, and gain enough knowledge on how to use it for the benefits of making her your wife.

Chapter-92

Personality Disfigurement

Psychological problems can be more than skin deep, depending on the state of mind that the person is in. This may or may not be a state of mind created at birth that sometimes makes a man or woman seem unattached to common sense or logic. By being mentally challenged in most cases while trying to live normal lives, which has become more defined since these people are dating in a self proclaimed atmosphere. Where cops are not the hero's . . . women are. It's not uncommon now a days when women are dating a man with some kind of existing mental issue. When the date turns ugly when he touches you where it is not allowed and you have noticed his behavior has completely changed from friendly to predator. You spring into action by spraying and emptying a can of mace in his face and running for help to the nearest place, or person you can find thus ending that psycho-date abruptly. These type of men are either very stupid with no home training or guidance on how to treat women while growing up as a child, or just a straight sociopath. A man wears his disguise when they are not sure of themselves or just simply afraid of being rejected by some lady he really wants; with thoughts that linger in his mind finding the only alternative which is to take what he likes. With all their individual indifferences women are finding it harder and harder to find a man of good quality. Concentrating on certain areas of men while trying to stay focused on what she is truly looking for without getting side tracked on the intricate parts of what make a meaningful relationship. The complexities of a man's own self worth is sometimes difficult to resolve or understand, unless that man understand himself. Most educated women can figure men out based on their personality and intellect knowing that all men are different. No matter what race each man has different characteristics traits and the ladies are what makes men so unique.

Chapter-93

Detachment Eye's

Split decision can be made at the blink of an eye, we try hard not to stare at someone that you like and want that peaks your interest to be your mate. Attractive women get men attention daily making them the center of attention whenever going about their routines, rather it's work or going to stores men always love looking at the beauty of a woman, and the magnificent ways she dresses. In doing so the man thats interested is hoping she notice him the way he feels about her. Men and women bare some of the same instincts when it comes to the opposites attract. When a woman is attracted to a man she will go out her way literally to get to know him especially if she's a single woman. Some might even break a nail or two getting a pen just so she can give him her phone number depending on the way he looks and dresses. Men are even worst when chasing behind women that they want, sometimes by doing silly things with leaps and bounds proven how much he want to meet her acquaintance. So when you see a beautiful lady walking by just simply say hello, and the rest will fall into place for a night on the town or for the sake of just simply having one date.

Chapter-94

Don't Be A Lost Soul

Comfort in our daily lives is what we seek through our everyday activities; which seem like a never ending task of refection of the things we do after a stressful day of working. Unwinding is not much less than creativity of relaxing other than trying to get a extra amount of sleep. Creativity also can fall into the category of sleeping with your best friends girl or for close encounters of sleeping with his or her sister. Whatever the case we all indulge sinful acts in some form or fashion, our promiscuous nature only separate those whom claim religious belief no matter what advances are practices. A lot of people may say that it's psychological to the extent of being in a different state of mind that an individual holds proposition or promises. How this defines a person depends on their mental state being, having acceptance by restoring a person sense of balance. A judgment call is normally measured by his or her ego depending on the person being judged, sometimes people can be so unrelenting in the way we exploit ourselves for our own financial and sexual gratifications. With each desire given of happiness and pain which is often time is followed by a endless supply of impulses, on a adventure with no interruption as if it were a race against time itself. Bringing all forces together in the lime light of dating where adventure take on a different episode by leaving what evil that trail right where you found it; while trying to rewrite the story of my life. A true introduction to change comes from the source itself, (you) no matter how noble with flaming cascading ideas. A man or woman should pick up a good romance novel that has certain appeal if you're trying to get close to someone you really like. This helps you to leave a imprint on the person you're dating offering them the world in order to relieve the pressure of love weighing heavily on their minds.

Chapter-95

If He Is Anything Like His Mother

When a woman dates a man that has been raised by his mother without the help of the father. Nine times out of ten he will inherit all of her emotional issues that his mother carries alone with the issues of distrust and all the burden of being a woman. Depending on how he was raised he can grow out of it and mature into the man he suppose to be. However, ladies if you're looking to have a long term relationship with these men. Make sure to take the necessary precautions; It might be in your best interest to do an analysis on the guy you're dating in order to get a better understanding who he is while getting a second opinion on what you have learned. What I mean by this is when you meet his mother see if she is a compassionate person nice or mean. If the man you are dating has no mother or father around ask about his upbringing and how he was raised. If he does, then it just might be him, in his attitude in the act of his behavior with all accountability belonging to him.

Chapter-96

Don't Date A Flunky Punk Man

The majority of these type of men are gay, booty lovers to the fullest. With their tight clothes and funny looking hairstyles makes a normal mans stomach turn with aw. These servants of the devil that perform nasty unquestionable acts of sex, that leaves each to his own with a new meaning. Some of it I wouldn't even dare mention, and don't care to for the fear of making you gag. Some of these gay guys go for women and men as if they are trying to sympathize with the facts that they are doing society a favor, with their scandaless behavior. Accepting all acts of taking advantage of the women being mislead in thinking that the guy she is dating is normal. Having no self remorse for what they do when infecting these women with H.I.V. This is a trend that has spread faster than cancer, when the only red flag pops up is when it is too late to do anything when the damage has already been done. This has become one of the worst conditions of dating making it even harder for the straight men to express themselves without women wanting to know if he has slept with another man. Making it even more embarrassing for women asking the question which becomes a matter of life and death; when the only thing she is trying to do is date a normal man she is looking to have a lifetime relationship with. The very idea of gays behavior makes me cringe, because they are like some plague of an infectious disease that's made it's way into homes of decent people spreading the aids virus. I guess that's putting it mildly when the term flunky punk men are used instead of the keywords like faggots, punks, gays, or homosexuals. However, a person describes them I simply don't approve.

Chapter-97

Male Jackasses With Large Ego's

A man that do foolish, stupid, and silly things is known as a jackass contrary to popular demand. If he does not treat women accordingly when they are on a date, he is consider as being very irrational because of his lack of respect for the opposite sex. Thus labeling him a (jackass) when considering the term which is a stubborn mule that has the horse for a mother and a donkey for a father. Making it less than the actual horse of what it is intended to be, by making it less of a thoroughbred in fact of being a jackass. Hypothetically speaking the human race is not much different when you're looking at it from a geographical stand point. In retrospect we as human beings have some of the same characteristics traits no matter the region of planet earth we are on. There's a jackass found on all of them, these type of men that are only out to sleep with each and every woman they can in order to gain status with the self satisfaction that he did. Making them feel superior in merit of the number of women that they plugged, when women are very fragile with emotion in thoughts. How you deal with these type of guy's with large ego's you don't, because in every aspect of dating from what I have seen he is pretty much what a woman wants.

Chapter-98

Twisted Sista's

All drama no bull these women have a endless supply of mess, white or black it don't matter they have huge personality disorder. The majority of these women are in constant denial about what they want, how they want it, and what they do. Some of these women on these dating sites don't seem to have no clue, and don't try to make sense out of some of the answers they give because it just might confuse you. Anything to do with logic is followed by a attitude when asking a simple question about her back ground and if she has kids, they act as if it was a foolish question or you just broke a rule. Despite the conversation you might relay to her with messages back and forth, on different and certain topics in knowing who they are. Trying to see if she is compatible enough and sane to be your mate. You must tread lightly and be careful of what you say, because a lot of women get it twisted on what they think they heard. While refusing to acknowledge the facts that they might have a problem, and maybe they need to find a method to see if they can solve it.

Chapter-99

Those Guy's With Pants Sagging

Did you know that the majority of young guy's that have their pants sagging have no idea where it originated from? They think just because it looks cool or it is what the rest of the so call gangsters are doing. That it makes them hard or tough to say the least that they are following the footsteps of gays. Well my unaware friends it came from gays in prisons while trying to get the attention of the other inmates. That they were interested in by pulling their paints down exposing the shape of their butts, in their boxer shorts to be fucked in their nasty ass. Some of the punks, faggs, gays whatever you choose to call them had their paints to go as low as beneath the butt cheeks along the hilt of their thigh's. How most young ladies find these guy's attractive of this manner leaves me baffled, maybe not knowing that the guy she is falling in love with likes other men too. That's where pants sagging come from ladies; and the majority of men that dress like that nine times out ten likes or love the ass's of other men. So next time you see that guy calling his self being cool with his pants sagging as if he is some kind of gangster, remember that he is classified as a booty bandit that likes other men.

Chapter-100

Don't Date
The Bottom Of The Barrel

This is the moment of truth where Carl Lewis the track star couldn't bring it to you any faster. Men with so many hang ups and draw backs if he was hanging off the side of a cliff, attached to a cable being pulled up by a crane he couldn't be lifted. These types of men have so many mental issues and symptoms a psychiatrist couldn't diagnose it. Most women don't see or recognize a man's problems until its too late, all the signs are there but unless he expresses his emotion a woman would never know it. We express ourselves through communication in order to have a understanding of the lessons we are trying to learn. We recognize our problems by past experiences expressing our emotion by signs left behind from bad behavior. When things don't go our way rather it's our financial dilemmas, or guilt from doing a girlfriend wrong because you're not able to provide some of the necessities a woman looks to have from a man. This doesn't give a man the right to mistreat a woman. Women use to having a strong devotion to support the man she is dating with some sense of direction in helping him out of a financial bind; depending on his character when he is hard pressed on placing the blame on things he cannot achieve. It becomes a condition of the mind when we place the blame on other people from situation we put ourselves into, and start hurting the person that's closest to us because you're suffering from loser syndrome. Making a change starts from within, if a man is willing to take a look at his self; to be a better a person in dating women that likes it when a man can hold his own. Any man that disrespects a woman while they are in process of getting to know each other when dating, don't deserve to be call a man at all, but a disease of sorts that can be mostly found at the garbage dump in a cesspool full of shit at bottom of a barrel.